WRITTEN BY:
LAUREN CHANDLER   CATALINA

Goodbye

PACKED WITH PUZZLES AND ACTIVITIES!

to GOODBYES

Art and activity book

Can you draw some more
people at the party?

Mary

thegoodbook
for children

Goodbye to Goodbyes Art and Activity Book
© The Good Book Company 2019

"The Good Book For Children" is an imprint of The Good Book Company Ltd
North America: www.thegoodbook.com UK: www.thegoodbook.co.uk
Australia: www.thegoodbook.com.au New Zealand: www.thegoodbook.co.nz
India: www.thegoodbook.co.in

Created and illustrated by André Parker, based on original illustrations by Catalina Echeverri

ISBN: 9781784983864 | Printed in India

In the little town of Bethany,
there lived a man named Lazarus.

He had two sisters, Mary and Martha.

Lazarus

Jesus

Martha

They were all friends with
a man named Jesus.

But one day,
Lazarus got sick.

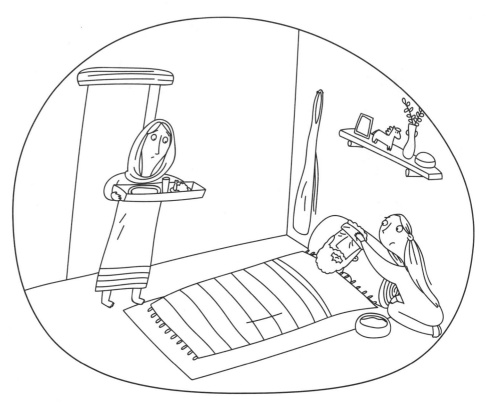

Martha and Mary
looked after him,

but Lazarus got worse
and worse...

"I know," said Martha,
"I will tell our friend Jesus!
He can help!"

So she and Mary sent a message to Jesus:

Lord Jesus,
   Our brother Lazarus,
the friend that you love,
   is sick.
      Come quickly!

Wordsearch

h	k	k	i	s	l	s	s	j	i	s	a	j	d	u
g	h	a	t	z	i	f	s	u	e	p	q	b	l	y
e	f	r	i	e	n	d	t	h	t	s	r	g	a	d
l	w	l	i	a	s	w	e	s	l	l	u	e	z	v
b	e	t	h	a	n	y	s	b	g	e	e	s	a	t
s	e	o	i	e	k	k	r	s	t	t	l	d	r	b
r	d	w	m	e	k	e	y	m	o	t	s	u	u	k
m	o	b	o	a	y	n	o	r	l	e	i	d	s	a
e	k	h	u	r	n	o	w	l	e	r	k	e	d	w
s	l	x	a	f	r	c	k	s	t	a	s	c	p	n
s	v	m	g	e	s	y	j	e	s	u	i	m	y	d
a	i	i	a	h	o	b	w	p	g	e	c	s	k	n
g	b	m	a	r	t	h	a	g	f	s	k	o	w	n
e	o	n	e	t	t	e	l	o	y	e	j	o	i	l
s	u	e	j	e	s	u	x	g	r	i	t	r	f	a

- [ ] Mary
- [ ] Martha
- [ ] Lazarus
- [ ] sick
- [ ] worry
- [ ] friend
- [ ] wrote
- [ ] letter
- [ ] Bethany
- [ ] town
- [ ] message
- [ ] Jesus

It took two days for Martha's
message to reach Jesus.

Can you follow
the path the
letter took?

Then for two whole days, Jesus
stayed right where he was.

Jesus told his disciples,
   "Our friend Lazarus is very sick.
But this illness won't end with Lazarus being dead.
We won't have to say goodbye forever. I have a plan."

Spot the difference

Can you spot the five differences between these two pictures?

At last, Jesus and his disciples
headed to Bethany.

Dead?! How could this be?
Didn't Jesus say that Lazarus would not die?
What happened to his plan?

Match the shadows

These people are all from the story.
Can you match them to their shadows?

Maze

Four days after Lazarus had died,
Jesus and his disciples finally arrived.
Martha came running to meet them.

a   b

c

Which path leads
Jesus to Martha?

"Lord!" she gasped. "If only you had been here, Lazarus would not have died. But I Know nothing is impossible with you — even after someone's died and we've said our forever goodbyes."

"You're right, Martha," Jesus said. "There is a day coming when we will say goodbye to saying goodbyes forever.

Maze

When they reached Lazarus's tomb,
Jesus cried too.

Can you find
the path to the
tomb?

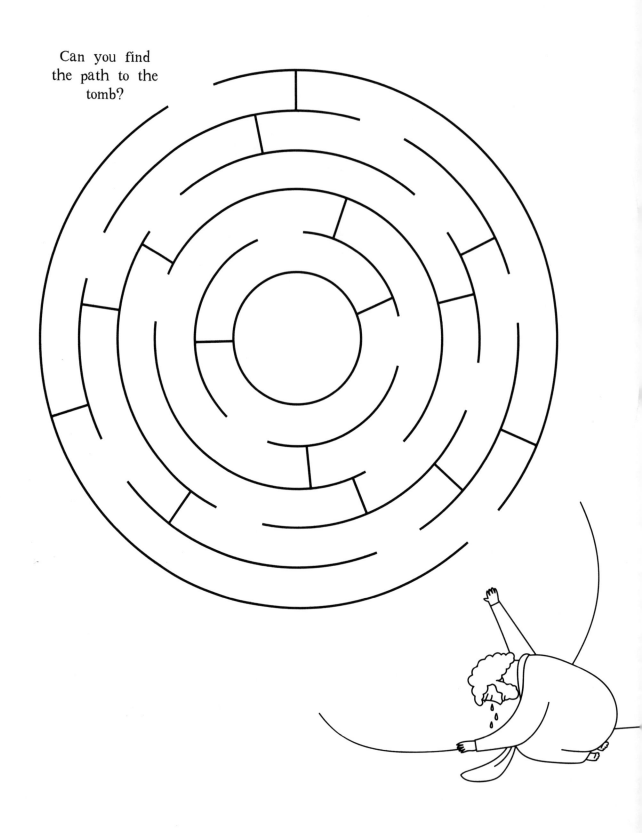

But then Jesus stopped crying and said...

Join the dots

Start at 1 and join the dots
to finish the picture

Now decorate
your picture!

They took away the stone, and Jesus
yelled, like a lion's mighty roar,

"Lazarus, come out!"

And...
he...

...did!

Wordsearch

r	K	i	g	b	h	s	a	g	e	s	c	u	y	u
e	d	c	t	r	l	y	t	p	l	a	e	p	r	y
m	i	i	c	o	f	t	r	h	l	r	p	o	f	d
e	s	r	d	o	g	z	t	r	o	a	y	l	o	v
m	c	r	y	e	r	e	s	l	h	a	n	d	r	t
b	i	o	i	i	a	r	t	a	d	a	l	i	e	b
t	p	l	t	o	m	b	p	h	o	r	d	y	v	K
n	l	i	r	i	s	h	e	y	e	y	s	r	e	s
l	e	l	u	e	s	y	t	l	i	r	i	t	r	t
a	s	x	r	e	b	K	K	s	o	r	s	t	b	o
z	j	h	j	d	r	u	i	r	e	e	d	m	e	n
s	a	o	o	a	p	a	l	i	v	e	a	s	r	e
e	j	o	u	r	n	e	y	g	o	t	i	c	i	e
g	g	t	e	h	e	r	u	i	e	f	g	i	r
s	f	o	y	t	h	a	s	a	d	s	a	b	f	b

- ☐ goodbye
- ☐ plan
- ☐ disciples
- ☐ journey
- ☐ forever
- ☐ sad
- ☐ tomb
- ☐ stone
- ☐ cry
- ☐ alive
- ☐ happy
- ☐ together

A happy ending

How does Martha feel now?
Put a ✓ next to the right face:

Jesus Kept his word.
Lazarus being sick didn't end with him being dead.
It ended with him alive even after he died —
after they'd had to say goodbye!

Finish this picture by adding lots more people to the party!

Now decorate your picture!

Mary, Martha, Lazarus, and Jesus were together again.

Jesus Knows it is sad to say goodbye.
So Jesus came to end goodbyes.

And one day, Jesus and all his friends will say
goodbye to goodbyes — forever!

Use these pages to draw your very best picture of heaven! Fill it with lots and lots of happy people who have said goodbye to goodbyes!

Answers

Wordsearch 1

h	k	k	i	s	l	s	s	j	i	s	a	j	d	u
g	h	a	t	z	i	f	s	u	e	p	q	b	l	y
e	f	r	i	e	n	d	t	h	t	s	r	g	a	d
l	w	l	i	a	s	w	e	s	l	l	u	e	z	v
b	e	t	h	a	n	y	s	b	g	e	e	s	a	t
s	e	o	i	e	K	K	r	s	t	t	l	d	r	b
r	d	w	m	e	K	e	y	m	o	t	s	u	u	K
m	o	b	o	a	y	n	o	r	l	e	i	d	s	a
e	K	h	u	r	n	o	w	l	e	r	k	e	d	w
s	l	x	a	f	r	c	K	s	t	a	s	c	p	n
s	v	m	g	e	s	y	j	e	s	u	i	m	y	d
a	i	i	a	h	o	b	w	p	g	e	c	s	K	n
g	b	m	a	r	t	h	a	g	f	s	K	o	w	n
e	o	n	e	t	t	e	l	o	y	e	j	o	i	l
s	u	e	j	e	s	u	x	g	r	i	r	f	a	

Spot the difference

Maze 1

Match the shadows

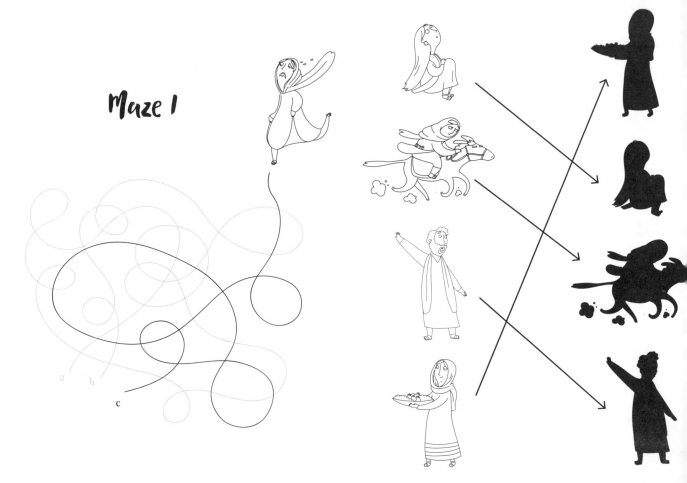

Maze 2

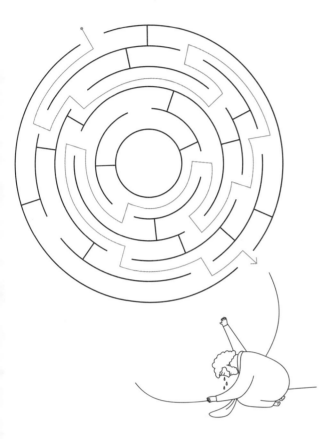

Wordsearch 2

r	K	i	g	b	h	s	a	g	e	s	c	u	y	u
e	d	c	t	r	l	y	t	p	l	a	e	p	r	y
m	i	i	c	o	f	t	r	h	l	r	p	o	f	d
e	s	r	d	o	g	z	K	r	o	a	y	l	o	v
m	c	r	y	e	r	e	s	l	h	a	n	d	r	t
b	i	o	i	i	a	r	t	a	d	a	l	i	e	b
t	p	l	t	o	m	b	p	h	o	r	d	y	v	k
n	l	i	r	i	s	h	e	y	e	y	s	r	e	s
l	e	l	u	e	s	y	t	l	i	r	i	t	r	t
a	s	x	r	e	b	K	K	s	o	r	s	t	b	o
z	j	h	j	d	r	u	i	r	e	e	d	m	e	n
s	a	o	o	a	p	a	l	i	v	e	a	s	r	e
e	j	o	u	r	n	e	y	g	o	t	i	c	i	e
g	t	e	t	h	e	r	u	i	e	f	g	i	r	
s	f	o	y	t	h	a	s	a	d	s	a	b	f	b

Join the dots

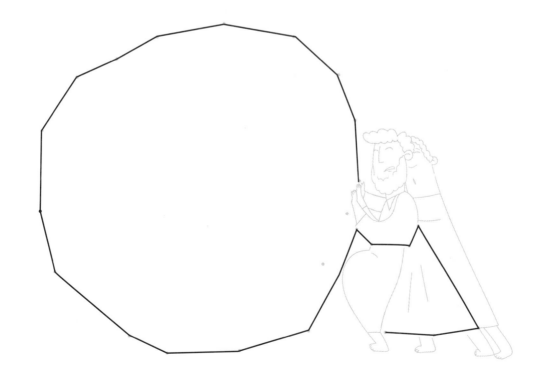

Now read the book!

If you enjoyed this activity book, read the full story in "Goodbye to Goodbyes."

Other books available in the award-winning "Tales That Tell The Truth" series:

www.thegoodbook.com

www.thegoodbook.co.uk